DISCARDED
From Nashville Public Library
Property of
Nashville Public Library
615 Church St., Nashville, Tn. 37219

LATINOS IN THE LIMELIGHT

Christina Aguilera
Antonio Banderas
Jeff Bezos
Oscar De La Hoya
Cameron Diaz
Scott Gomez
Salma Hayek
Enrique Iglesias

John Leguizamo
Jennifer Lopez
Ricky Martin
Pedro Martinez
Freddie Prinze Jr.
Selena
Carlos Santana
Sammy Sosa

CHELSEA HOUSE PUBLISHERS

LATINOS
IN THE
LIMELIGHT

Pedro Martinez

Stephen Krasner

CHELSEA HOUSE PUBLISHERS
Philadelphia

Frontis: Pedro Martinez, superstar pitcher for the Boston Red Sox, is a fierce competitor on the pitching mound.

CHELSEA HOUSE PUBLISHERS

Editor in Chief: Sally Cheney
Director of Production: Kim Shinners
Production Manager: Pamela Loos
Art Director: Sara Davis
Production Editor: Diann Grasse
Editor: Bill Conn

Layout by
21st Century Publishing and Communications, Inc.
http://www.21cpc.com

© 2002 by Chelsea House Publishers, a subsidiary of
Haights Cross Communications. All rights reserved.
Printed and bound in the United States of America.

The Chelsea House World Wide Web address is
http://www.chelseahouse.com

First Printing

1 3 5 7 9 8 6 4 2

CIP applied for ISBN 0-7910-6480-8

Contents

CHAPTER 1
"THE LEGEND OF PEDRO"   7

CHAPTER 2
MY BROTHER, MY HERO   17

CHAPTER 3
A CELEBRITY IN
THE DOMINICAN REPUBLIC   27

CHAPTER 4
NO MVP AWARD?   37

CHAPTER 5
THE TWO SIDES OF PEDRO   45

CHAPTER 6
CAN YOU TOP THIS?   53

CHRONOLOGY   59
ACCOMPLISHMENTS   61
FURTHER READING   61
INDEX   62

1

"The Legend of Pedro"

Pedro Martinez, superstar pitcher for the Boston Red Sox, walked into the team's dugout at Jacobs Field in Cleveland on October 11, 1999. He was not alone. Pedro was followed by the team's physician, the team's trainer, the manager, several players, and a large number of media members.

They all watched with concerned looks on their faces as Pedro picked up his glove and a baseball, and walked out onto the field to play catch. On any normal day in baseball, this is a routine activity. But this wasn't a normal day. And there was nothing routine about Pedro Martinez playing catch on this particular day.

Only five days earlier, Pedro had felt a "pinch" in his back while pitching in the first game against the Cleveland Indians in the best-of-five series in the first round of the American League playoffs. That "pinch," a muscle strain just below his right shoulder, forced him out of the game early.

After taking medicine and receiving medical treatment over the next few days, Pedro wanted to pitch again.

The Red Sox and the Cleveland Indians were preparing

Fighting through the pain of an injury with sheer determination and a competitive spirit, Pedro led the Boston Red Sox to the American League Championship Series with a victory over the Cleveland Indians in 1999.

to play the deciding fifth game of their series. Cleveland won the first two games of the series. Boston won the next two games. The winner on this night would advance to the next round of the playoffs, the American League Championship Series, to play the New York Yankees. And Pedro, even though he knew he wouldn't be able to give 100 percent, wanted to help his teammates.

As Pedro started to loosen up and play catch, the number one question of the evening wasn't, "Who will win the game?" No, the question was, "Is Pedro healthy enough to pitch?" About six hours later, the Red Sox, their fans, and a national television audience had the answer to that important question.

Pedro, through sheer determination, competitive desire, and consummate skill, ignored any pain and stiffness in his back and gave one of the most courageous, heroic pitching performances in playoff history.

Pedro entered the game in the fourth inning with the score tied at 8-8. He pitched the next six innings and did not allow any runs. Indeed, he didn't give up any hits and he struck out eight batters as the Red Sox beat the powerful Indians, 12-8, and advanced to the American League Championship Series.

Pedro's fastball, which usually lit up the radar gun at 95 and 96 miles an hour, barely made it up to 90 miles an hour on that night. But even without his best fastball, Pedro still found a way to dominate the Cleveland Indians, who had one of the best offensive teams in baseball.

"Pedro was hot today," said Omar Vizquel, Cleveland's shortstop, after the game. "It didn't matter if he had a bad shoulder or a bad

"THE LEGEND OF PEDRO"

Pedro throws the final pitch for a strikeout in the Red Sox' win over the Indians in the 1999 AL Division Series. Even with an injured back, Pedro struck out eight batters and didn't give up any hits.

whatever. He showed you what he has: a great heart."

Pedro is not a big man. He stands only 5' 11" and weighed about 165 pounds on that night in Cleveland. But he was strong enough to carry the win for the Red Sox on his back.

"It felt a little tighter in the last two innings," admitted Pedro after the victory, referring to the injured muscle in his back. "[B]ut I guess the adrenaline at that point, and knowing that we had the lead and knowing that I had to make sure we kept the lead, I guess I was getting a little stronger. I wasn't going to let go."

So there was Pedro, after starring in the middle in the baseball diamond, standing in the middle of the Red Sox' boisterous clubhouse, with loud salsa music blaring from a stereo, being mobbed by his appreciative teammates.

The joyous scene provided a huge contrast to the mood in that very same clubhouse only five days earlier. At that point, Pedro was downcast, feeling pain in his back. The Red Sox were just as down, having lost their best player, seriously hurting their hopes for a victory in the playoff series. Professional sports can be a roller coaster of emotions.

For Pedro, the 1999 regular season provided mostly "highs" with only a few "lows" tossed in. Pedro won 23 games, the most in the American League. He lost only 4 games. Pedro led the league by striking out 313 batters. His 313 strikeouts also set a Boston Red Sox record. And he also led the league in a statistic called "earned-run average." Pedro allowed only 2.07 earned runs per game.

The only problem Pedro had during the regular season was in late July, when he had a sore right shoulder, an injury that forced him onto the team's disabled list, keeping him out of action for 15 days.

In general, when Pedro pitched, the Red Sox, with good reason, expected to win. So when the playoff series against Cleveland was about to begin, the Red Sox felt good about their chances.

Manager Jimy Williams sent Pedro out to pitch Game One of the playoff series. Over the first three innings, Pedro gave up three hits, but no runs. Boston was ahead, 2-0.

In the fourth inning, though, there was a

problem for Pedro and the Red Sox. Ironically, the problem came on a 96 mile-an-hour fastball that struck out Jim Thome for the first out of the inning. "I felt a burning sensation in my back," Pedro would say later. He got the next two batters out, but it was clear something was wrong. His fastball was registering only 88 miles an hour. Catcher Jason Varitek noticed Pedro wasn't himself. Pitching coach Joe Kerrigan noticed it, and so did Pedro's older brother, Ramon, who also pitched for the Red Sox.

Pedro wanted to continue. That was the competitor in him, but deep down, he knew better. He realized that he had to come out of the game. "I wasn't going to be stupid about it," said Pedro. "I didn't want to mess around with it. . . . I just felt it on one pitch. It could happen at any time. It could have been [caused by] the cold [it was 49 degrees at game time], but I don't know. It could have been an over-juiced fastball."

Pedro was worried that this pain was related to his shoulder problem in July. Team physician Dr. William Morgan assured him it wasn't. This time, it was a muscle just below his right shoulder.

Nevertheless, Pedro was out of the game. His chances of being able to pitch later in the series didn't look good, even if Boston was able to extend the series by winning two games. It was the team's worst nightmare. "We're really worried about Pedro," said third baseman John Valentin after the team lost that night, 3-2. "He basically got us [into the playoffs]."

Pedro, meanwhile, talked bravely about being able to come back. "Don't scare our fans," said Pedro. "Don't bring any negative stuff out to our fans, because I'm going to be back in the house." By "back in the house," Pedro meant back on the mound. But privately, he wasn't so sure. There were many times after the game that night that Pedro asked himself, "Why me?" and "Why now?"

Fortunately for Pedro, he was able to talk things out with his older brother, Ramon. "Yeah, he was feeling that way," said Ramon. "But it's part of the game. He was upset when he came out of the game. But when we got to the hotel room, we relaxed a bit. We talked for a long time." There was nothing for Pedro to do but take his medication, undergo treatment, and hope he'd heal quickly enough to help his teammates if needed.

When Boston lost Game Two, 11-1, it looked as if the Sox were in trouble. One more loss and the season would be over. Pedro tried playing catch before Game Three, but the pain caused him to stop trying after only about a dozen throws. Still, he was hoping to be ready if a decisive Game Five were necessary.

For their part, the Red Sox made sure a Game Five was necessary. Boston rebounded in the series, beating Cleveland by 9-3 in Game Three, and then moved on to a 23-7 victory in Game Four. The Red Sox were alive. But was Pedro ready to help?

When he got to the ballpark on October 11, Pedro wasn't sure if he would be able to play. He wanted to tell his body to be ready and to ignore any pain, just for this one game.

It was clear that the Red Sox would not be able to count on him for a full nine innings. But even if they could have him for even two or three innings, they would be happy. There

"The Legend of Pedro"

Pedro beats a Cleveland Indian to first base for an out during Game 5 of the playoffs, showing both fans and teammates alike what it means to be a tough competitor.

he was, in the dugout, picking up his glove and a baseball and walking onto the field. He made a few tosses. He got loose. There was discomfort, but Pedro masked the pain well. He threw a few pitches, again masking any pain he might have been feeling so his manager and pitching coach would allow him to pitch, if needed.

Pedro claimed to be fine after his test. Still, the Sox were hoping they could win without him, so their valuable pitcher wouldn't run the risk of further injuring himself. But the game wasn't going well for the Red Sox. They were scoring plenty of runs, but they couldn't keep the Indians from scoring. So manager Jimy Williams and pitching coach Joe Kerrigan turned to Pedro.

Once again Pedro grabbed his glove. This time he ran to the Red Sox bullpen and warmed up.

When he came into the game, it was tied at 8-8 entering the bottom of the fourth inning. Jimy Williams and Joe Kerrigan only hoped Pedro could throw 40 pitches. They didn't think his body would allow him more work. They were wrong. Pedro set down all three batters in the fourth inning. He struck out two batters in the fifth. He had thrown 36 pitches already. But he refused to come out. Pedro struck out two more batters in the sixth, pushing his pitch count to 57. But still, he refused to come out. "I decided I was the one that had to be out there," Pedro would say later. "I wasn't thinking about coming out."

In the top of the seventh, Boston's Troy O'Leary hit a three-run home run, giving the Red Sox an 11-8 lead. There was no way that Pedro was coming out. The competitive fire burned too fiercely within him. He lived for such challenges.

Pedro got two more strikeouts in the seventh and another one in the eighth. And, after the Red Sox pushed across another run in the ninth, Pedro Martinez retired all three batters he faced in the final inning, polishing off his game by striking out Omar Vizquel for the last out.

Pedro Martinez threw 97 pitches in spite of his pain. In some ways, he even surprised himself.

Pedro's joyous teammates spray him with champagne in celebration of their Game victory over the Cleveland Indians, which gave the Red Sox a spot in the 1999 American League Division Championships.

"I had doubts," said Pedro. "But once I stepped on the mound, I never did. I wanted to get the adrenaline going and get the mind going and hopefully, that would drive me to just throw the ball over the plate and see what I could do."

He did a lot. It wasn't just that Pedro Martinez won the game. It was how he virtually willed himself to pitch a great game, against one of the best-hitting teams in baseball, that inspired awe in all who were fortunate enough to have seen the superb performance.

"It's one of the most heroic, gutsy performances I've ever seen," said pitching coach Joe Kerrigan. "Here's a guy who wasn't supposed to pitch tonight except for an inning or two. And here he is throwing [about] 100 pitches.

Kerrigan said in admiration, "The legend of Pedro."

2

MY BROTHER, MY HERO

The Martinez brothers didn't need any uniforms, nor did they need any fancy scoreboards. The boys didn't require a perfectly laid out baseball diamond with the grass beautifully manicured. They didn't even need official baseball bats. The Martinez brothers only needed some kind of ball, maybe a rubber ball, or a tennis ball, or a real baseball if they should be lucky enough to get their hands on one.

As for a baseball bat, often a tree limb freshly cut down from somewhere near a field in their home town of Manoguayabo in the Dominican Republic would work just fine on those days when their teams in organized youth leagues weren't playing. Almost every day, the Martinez brothers — Nelson, Ramon, Pedro, and Jesus — would play baseball.

They had a lot of fun playing baseball. Nelson and Pedro usually played together as a team against Ramon and Jesus. They had fun, but they were also very competitive. "Sometimes we'd argue," said Ramon with a laugh. "Not that much. About a pitch sometimes. 'That was a strike.'

The perfect form Pedro displays here on the mound was developed in the competitive baseball games he would play with his brothers in the Dominican Republic.

'No, it wasn't. It was a ball.'" Pedro added, "It was always fun. It was so neat."

Baseball was a passion for the Martinez brothers, and it carried three of them all the way from the hot fields of Manoguayabo to professional baseball in the United States. Nelson, the oldest, never signed with a major league organization, but Ramon, the second-oldest, Pedro, and Jesus, the youngest, did.

Ramon, who is four years older than Pedro, signed with the Los Angeles Dodgers in 1984 and made it to the major leagues to stay in 1990. He won 20 games that year, and eventually pitched in All-Star Games and even pitched a no-hitter in 1995.

Pedro watched his brother carefully. And Pedro talked to Ramon all the time about pitching, about life, and about professional baseball as his older brother's major league career took off.

Pedro wanted to learn as much as he could about everything, and as fast as he could. Pedro was a student, seeking knowledge from Ramon, and Ramon was happy to pass on whatever knowledge he had gained.

Although the two of them were different in personality and body type, both were intelligent and humble individuals.

Ramon grew to be 6' 4" and weighed about 185 pounds. He was quiet by nature and not all that comfortable in the spotlight. Pedro, on the other hand, was about 5' 11" and weighed about 180 pounds. He was the family jokester, a personality that didn't change when he became a star in the big leagues. The family bond, though, was always strong.

In 1988 it looked as though Ramon and

Pedro would get the chance to reawaken their boyhood memories, when they played together. That dream arose when the Los Angeles Dodgers signed Pedro to a professional contract. Pedro was beginning his career in Great Falls, Montana, in 1990.

As Pedro was pitching his way through the Dodgers' minor-league system, through stops in Bakersfield, California; San Antonio, Texas; and Albuquerque, New Mexico, he studied hard, not only on the field, but also in the classroom. Pedro learned English quickly and became comfortable with the language.

Pedro's talents were making him a top prospect for the major league. In 1991 The Sporting News named Pedro the Minor League Player of the Year. In 1992 he was selected to pitch in the Triple A All-Star Game, and Baseball America named him the 10th best prospect in all of the minor leagues. Triple A is just one level below the major leagues.

By then, Ramon was a star. Still, he kept his eye out for his younger brother. "When I came up to the major leagues (in 1988, at the age of 20), I was set on the target of getting to the major leagues," said Ramon. "You have to work hard. That's what I taught him. And I told him to be competitive, be the most competitive. I saw when he was growing up how competitive he was."

"I would tell him a lot of things he didn't know yet about the game, how to take care of himself, things about the hitters," said Ramon. "I kept track of him when he was in the minor leagues. I heard a lot of good things about him."

Pedro, meanwhile, was feeling the effects of

Whether playing baseball as boys in the Dominican Republic or as professionals together on the Boston Red Sox, Pedro has always described his older brother, Ramon, as his idol and his hero.

Ramon's shadow that was being cast all the way from Los Angeles to those minor league cities where he pitched.

It was hard for Pedro to be known as Ramon's younger brother, especially because of the differences in their size. "A lot of people made jokes," recalled Pedro. "They looked at me and saw me so small they never thought I could perform at (the major league) level. And it was like, 'He might be here because he's Ramon's little brother.'"

Pedro's performance on the field was also

compared to Ramon's minor league performance. "I took the mound and did whatever I did and they always looked for the numbers that Ramon put up in the minor leagues and compared them to mine. I thought that wasn't fair. Sometimes they said Ramon's younger brother is coming up, he might be as good. But I was only in rookie (first-year) ball (in 1990). Ramon was pitching in the All-Star Game. I didn't like that. I wanted to be Pedro. The one and only Pedro. I wanted to be my own person," said Pedro.

Even though Pedro didn't like being compared to Ramon, it was Pedro's dream to pitch on the same team as his brother. Pedro made that happen by winning games and striking out batters in the minors. In 1992, after going 7-6 and striking out 124 batters in 125 innings for Albuquerque, the Dodgers' top minor league team, Pedro was promoted to Los Angeles.

This was the beginning of some happy times for Pedro and Ramon in L.A. Pedro pitched in only two games that summer for the Dodgers, once taking over in a game Ramon had started. But in 1993, Pedro went 10-5 in 65 games for the Dodgers, pitching mostly in relief.

Pedro, though, always wanted to be a starting pitcher, like his brother. He was confident he had the ability to pitch nine innings on a regular basis, and not just one or two here and there. The Dodgers, however, were afraid that Pedro was too frail to hold up for an entire season. They thought there was a strong possibility the right-hander's pitching arm would get hurt, unable to withstand the wear and tear that comes with throwing 200 innings a year as a starting pitcher. The Dodgers weren't even convinced that Pedro's arm would hold up in a role as a relief pitcher.

The dream of being on the same team as his brother, which had become a reality for Pedro and Ramon, did not last. The Dodgers shattered it by trading Pedro to the Montreal Expos after the 1993 season for a second baseman named Delino DeShields. Pedro was crushed.

Ramon once again played the role of older, wiser brother, as he had done throughout Pedro's life. Ramon told Pedro how it was time for him to be on his own, to be out from under his older brother's shadow. Ramon explained to Pedro how in Montreal he would be able to develop his own identity.

Ramon reassured Pedro that he was going to be a good pitcher and that pitching in Montreal was a golden opportunity for him to prove to himself. He would be able to show the Dodgers and the rest of the baseball world that he was strong enough and talented enough to be a winning pitcher in the major leagues. Pedro listened. He tried to understand, but his heart hurt too much from being traded away from his brother.

Pedro eventually realized that Ramon was right. It took a while for Pedro to accept the trade, but playing in Montreal turned out to be the best thing for Pedro and his career. In four seasons with the Expos, Pedro won 55 games and lost only 33. In 1997 Pedro was 17-8, with an earned-run average of a spectacular 1.90, which was the best in the National League. He struck out 305 batters in only 241 innings that year.

MY BROTHER, MY HERO

Pedro was heartbroken at the thought of leaving his brother, Ramon, when he was traded from the L.A. Dodgers to the Montreal Expos. As his brother predicted, the trade was a golden opportunity for Pedro—at the end of his first season with the Expos he had earned the Cy Young Award, which is given to the best pitcher in the league.

When the season was over, the Baseball Writers Association of America voted him the Cy Young Award, given annually to the best pitcher in each league. By then Pedro knew the trade from the Dodgers to the Expos had been a positive career move. At that point, Pedro, only 26 years old, was regarded as one of baseball's best pitchers, and he was adored by the fans in Montreal.

He has since been able to reflect on the trade and appreciate Ramon's comments and advice when he was first told of the trade.

Pedro and Ramon made major league history when the Expos played the Dodgers in 1996, becoming the sixth set of brothers to start as pitchers on opposing teams.

Pedro said:

> I thought it would be better to keep me together with Ramon. And I cried and whined about it, how I wanted to play with my brother and how I missed my brother, how I didn't have anybody to talk to. But Ramon told me I shouldn't be afraid. Ramon was always able to make me feel like I was standing on the ground. After I played for a year and a half in Montreal, I realized it was better, but until then, I didn't believe it.

There was one stressful time between the brothers, however. On August 29, 1996, when the Dodgers played a game in Montreal, Ramon started for Los Angeles, and Pedro started for the Expos. It was only the sixth time in major league history that brothers had started in a game against each other. Pedro was feeling a mixture of emotions. "I didn't want to do bad because I didn't want to let him down and make him feel sorry for me, but at the same time I didn't want him to beat me," said Pedro.

Pedro struck out 12 Dodgers in a game that was emotional for each brother. But Ramon was the winning pitcher. Los Angeles beat Montreal, 2-1.

Pedro and Ramon would hook up again, after the 1998 season. Pedro had been traded to the Boston Red Sox prior to the 1999 season. Ramon, whose 1998 season was cut short by shoulder surgery, left the Dodgers and also signed with the Red Sox. "This is very special for me. I knew coming here would be a chance to play with Pedro," said Ramon when he signed his contract. Ramon and Pedro pitched together for the Boston Red Sox in 1999 and 2000. By then, Pedro's pitching skills had surpassed those of Ramon, who was trying to rebound from his shoulder surgery.

Pedro won the Cy Young Award in the American League in each of those seasons. But he never lost his respect and admiration for his older brother, Ramon.

"Ramon is pretty much everything I need," said Pedro one day during the 1999 season. "He is the reason I am what I am. He's my hero."

A Celebrity in the Dominican Republic

Pedro's contract with the Boston Red Sox was the largest in history at the time.

After acquiring Pedro Martinez from the Montreal Expos in a trade after the 1997 season, the Boston Red Sox wanted to make sure the talented right-handed pitcher, only 26 at the time, would stay with the Red Sox for a long time.

The 1998 season was the last remaining year on Pedro's contract, so the Red Sox offered Pedro an extension on that contract. The sides ultimately agreed on a six-year deal worth a total of $75 million, a contract that averaged out to $12.5 million a year. It was a staggering sum in baseball at the time, a contract that made Pedro Martinez the highest-paid pitcher in the game.

It was an especially staggering sum to a man who had grown up in the Dominican Republic, where so many people lived in poverty. Pedro wanted to share some of that wealth with the people of his hometown, Manoguayabo. The question was what could he do that would be special for them? It didn't take long for him

---

Pedro became the highest-paid pitcher in baseball when he signed a six-year deal worth $75 million in 1998. Pedro shared his wealth with his countrymen in the Dominican Republic by building a church in Manoguayabo, his hometown.

to come up with an answer.

At that time, Manoguayabo did not have a church to call its own. But now they do, thanks to Pedro's generosity. Pedro decided to have a church built in Manoguayabo.

It is not surprising that wherever Pedro goes at home he is mobbed, treated like royalty. Pedro is not famous just in Manoguayabo. Throughout the Dominican Republic, a small island roughly the size of West Virginia, Pedro is a hero.

Pedro has made it big. He has made it to the major leagues, and is living out the dream of scores of youngsters pursuing their passion for baseball on fields all over the largely poverty-stricken country.

Everyone wants to be like Pedro, or like other Dominican baseball stars such as Sammy Sosa. They want to use baseball as a way of leaving poverty behind, as a way in which they can make a living other than swinging a machete and cutting down sugar cane.

Wherever Pedro went he would be mobbed by young and old alike. Pedro's ready smile and easygoing nature would encourage others to just come up and say hello, ask for an autograph, or just settle for a firm handshake from one of the island's most famous celebrities.

If Pedro wanted to enjoy a little peace and quiet, he'd have to make definite plans to do so. "Sometimes I have to hide," said Pedro. "People wouldn't take 'No' for an answer."

One place where he could be at peace was at his mother's house in Hato Mayor, a rural village. Pedro and Ramon had the house built for her. It would be there, especially after a long, hard season, that Pedro would go to rest. "I play with the chickens, stay in a wooden house with no cable, no TV, just a little river passing by," said Pedro.

Pedro would return to the Dominican Republic after every season. And when he was home, while working out to get ready for the next major league season, he would see youngsters joyfully playing baseball. That would bring memories back to Pedro.

Pedro came by his love of baseball naturally, through his father, Paulino Jaime Abreu. When he was young, Abreu could usually be found on a field playing baseball.

Back then, though, there were no thoughts of playing major league baseball. There were no thoughts of earning $12.5 million a year just for throwing a baseball. Baseball was considered to be more of a hobby when Abreu was growing up.

"His mother told him his future was in farming. They understood baseball was just for fun," Pedro said. And just as it was for his father, that's what it was for Pedro and his brothers—fun. There were the neighborhood games, and there were also some supervised leagues that Pedro played in while he was growing up.

Pedro's parents were not wealthy. So when Pedro was chosen to participate on a Little League All-Star team that was going to play in the Little League World Series, he was unable to do so because his family couldn't afford the travel money. But there were many town tournaments during which Pedro would play for his town, Manoguayabo. One time, he hit a home run to win a game. Another time, he pitched 12 innings to win a game.

Pedro jokes with his former manager, Felipe Alou, from the Expos. When Pedro was growing up, he admired players like Alou who came from the Dominican Republic and made their mark on major league baseball.

He was a very intense competitor even then, admitting that there were times when he would get extremely upset if his team would lose a game.

While Pedro was growing up, a few players from the Dominican Republic began to make their marks in the major leagues. There were the Alou brothers—Felipe, Matty, and Jesus. There was a pitcher named Juan Marichal.

The country was hungry for heroes. Pedro's hero was Marichal, a right-handed pitcher who ultimately was voted into baseball's Hall of Fame, the first Dominican so honored. Felipe Alou, meanwhile, would become Pedro's manager in Montreal from 1994 to 1997.

Pedro wasn't the only one looking up to these stars. Baseball was as much a religion as it was a sport in the Dominican Republic. That was true when Pedro was a youngster, and it was still true when Pedro went back after the 1999 season.

"Go past any field and you'll see two teams playing and two teams waiting [to play]," said Pedro. Those fields would be crowded from the day's first light until late at night, with all ages represented. There would be amateur league games, pickup games, and youth league games. They would use whatever they could find to serve as a bat, a ball, or a glove. The winter baseball league in the Dominican Republic, which traditionally would feature several major leaguers, would be the focal point of the season.

Inside the Estadio Quisqueya in Santo Domingo, the capital of the Dominican Republic, fans would show their excitement and keep up with the action while the games were being played, eating fresh mango, corn on the cob, and fried plantains. Away from the stadium, though, conditions hadn't changed much since the time Pedro and his brothers would throw around a baseball.

The Dominican Republic is a very poor country, and the educational system is different than the system in the United States. There is a loosely run public education system, with most Dominican students not required to attend school after the sixth grade.

Jobs are not plentiful, either. Cutting down sugar cane with a machete along the roadside is one common job. The field where the Martinez brothers used to play baseball is now a juice factory that employs some Dominicans.

Pedro was very smart and always valued an education. He attended Ohio Dominican College in his native country. After he signed with the Los Angeles Dodgers, at the age of 16, Pedro took advantage of the school lessons the organization offered to its foreign players. Pedro attended English classes regularly and learned the language extremely well.

Pedro never forgot, however, where he came from, or how much he learned from his elders. When Pedro was voted his first Cy Young Award, while pitching for Montreal in 1997, signifying his status as the best pitcher in the National League that year, he gave the trophy to Juan Marichal, his boyhood hero.

Marichal, the country's Minister of Sport at the time, was impressed with Pedro's abilities and his intelligence. "The secret to pitching is to study hitters and throw the ball where they can't hit it, or at least to where they can't hit it hard," said Marichal, the first native of the Dominican Republic to make it into the Baseball Hall of Fame. "Pedro understands that," he said. "He studies everything he can about pitching."

Pedro's countrymen follow his career with a mixture of awe and hope, that maybe one day they, too, can leave the Dominican Republic for the riches of major league baseball.

Even when Pedro isn't around personally, he can be visible, as he was in March 2000. The Boston Red Sox and the Houston Astros, two major league teams that featured several Dominican natives, played two exhibition games in Santo Domingo, at Estadio Quisqueya. Pedro's appearance at the games was greatly

A Celebrity in the Dominican Republic

anticipated. Tied to one of the light towers in the outfield was a banner roughly 10 feet wide and 25 feet high. A picture of Pedro was on the banner, flashing his trademark smile. So even before he took the mound in the stadium, Pedro could be seen.

While he was in the country, Pedro visited the Red Sox' academy, a training facility for young Dominican players whom the organization thought might one day be good enough to play major league baseball.

Pedro poses in Fenway Park after a press conference shortly after signing his record-breaking deal with the Red Sox, thinking about how far he came from the poverty of the Dominican Republic and the life of farming that may have been his future.

Juan Marichal, the first Dominican to make it into the baseball Hall of Fame, gave hope to boys growing up in poverty in the Dominican Republic.

Pedro talked to the youngsters, telling them that their dreams could come true if they worked hard, just as he had when he was their age. "[These kids] have three times the drive that American kids have," said Pedro. "They want to become somebody. We've (Dominicans) got to be twice as good and have more drive. There are so many obstacles—the language, the culture, getting a visa. The kid from the Dominican has to push because (baseball) is the one chance he may get."

Pedro watched the kids working out. He didn't know any one of them very well, but in some ways, he did. Pedro could easily relate to their desire and their passion for the sport. "I see myself in every one of them," he said.

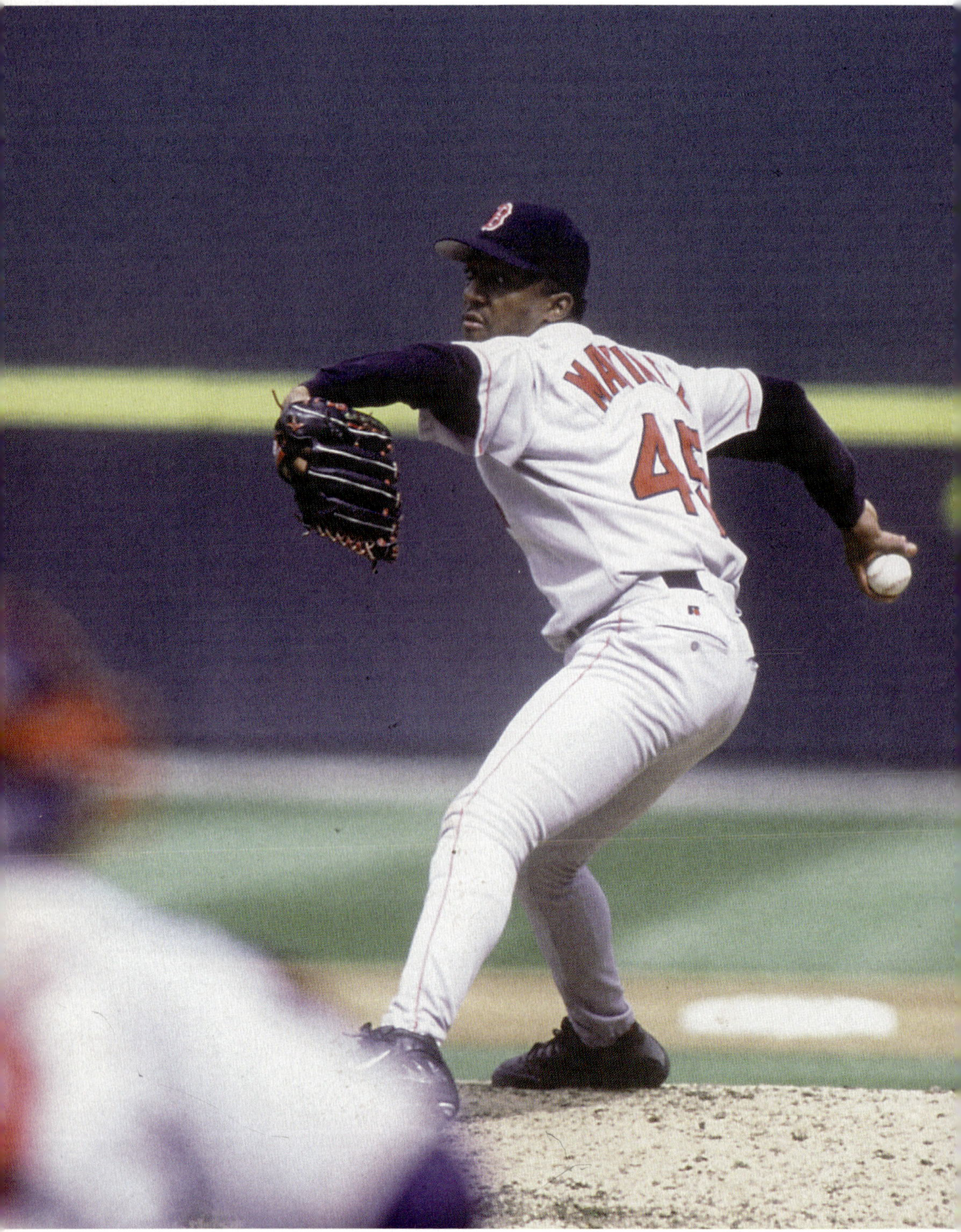

4

NO MVP AWARD?

The New York Yankees had won the World Series title in 1998. This was the team that was destined to win a second consecutive World Championship only about six weeks later. But when Pedro Martinez faced the Yankees on that magical night of September 10, 1999, in Yankee Stadium in the Bronx, he silenced New York's offense in a brilliant effort.

Pedro allowed only one hit—a solo home run by Chili Davis in the second inning—in pitching the Red Sox to an important 3-1 victory in front of 55,239 fans. The Yankee fans could do nothing by game's end but just admire the impressive performance being turned in against their heroes.

Davis was one of only two Yankees to reach base. Chuck Knoblauch, New York's leadoff hitter, had been hit with a pitch, but was thrown out trying to steal second base.

It was more than just a one-hitter, however. It was a masterpiece, as dominant a performance as had been seen in the major leagues in a long, long time. Pedro struck out 17 batters, a career high. The right-hander did not walk a batter. He ended the game by striking out the

---

In 1999 Pedro had one of the best pitching seasons in the history of the major leagues, leading the American League in wins, earned-run average, and strikeouts. If you ask his teammates, his biggest accomplishment is that he is always a team player.

final five batters he faced, and eight of the last nine. It was the most times a Yankee team had struck out in the history of the franchise.

Pedro mixed in his blazing 97-mile-an-hour fastballs, his deceptive changeup, and his sharp curveball in making the talented Yankees look feeble at the plate. It was a case of a man against boys, a concept not disputed after the game by the Yankees themselves.

"That's about as close to being unhittable as you can find," said Yankee manager Joe Torre. "The thing that was so impressive was he could have picked any pitch out of his pocket and thrown it for a strike."

"He's the best pitcher in baseball. Period," added Yankee right fielder Paul O'Neill.

Some people considered Pedro to be the best player in 1999. But this was not how he was seen by the Baseball Writers' Association of America, which votes for such postseason honors as the Most Valuable Player. Or, at least, not in the eyes of 2 of the 28 voters, who left Pedro off their ballots completely, not even giving him a second- or a third-place vote. If Pedro had been on those ballots, he could have won the Most Valuable Player Award in 1999 instead of Texas Rangers catcher Ivan "Pudge" Rodriguez. Pedro finished second, 13 points behind Rodriguez.

It's not as if those voters didn't think Pedro had been valuable in 1999. They were aware that Pedro had won 23 games and lost only 4. Voters knew that his earned-run average had been a relatively microscopic 2.07, meaning he had allowed only 2.07 earned runs for every nine innings he pitched. They also knew that he had struck out 313 batters during the season.

The writers reasoned that pitchers have their own honor, the Cy Young Award, which Pedro won unanimously. They thought the MVP should go to an everyday player, and not a starting pitcher, who generally works only once every five days. "I don't understand that, but I have no control over it," said Pedro of not winning the MVP vote.

What Pedro did have was amazing control of his three great pitches, so much control that it wasn't just the Yankees who felt as if it was futile to even try to hit against him.

In 1999, Pedro enjoyed one of the best seasons by a pitcher in the history of the major leagues. The numbers prove this fact. He led the American League in wins, earned-run average, and strikeouts, the first Red Sox pitcher to do so since the legendary Cy Young himself, in 1901.

Pedro also was named the league's Player of the Month four times, in April, May, June, and September, becoming the first player to ever win the award in three consecutive months. He struck out at least 10 batters in 19 of his 29 starts, fanning at least 10 in eight straight games, the first pitcher to do so in 22 years. And his 313 strikeouts established a Boston Red Sox single-season record.

Pedro accomplished these feats in the regular season. There were more career highlights in 1999.

Pedro was selected to his fourth All-Star Game, but this one was special. This one was held at Fenway Park, the home of Pedro's Boston Red Sox. And not only was Pedro chosen for the team, he was picked to start the game by Joe Torre, who was managing the American League team.

Fans tape up placards bearing the letter "K" for every strikeout he throws during the 1999 All-Star Game in Fenway Park.

The honor that went along with starting the game that features the best players in baseball was heady enough. Starting the game in front of an adoring home crowd that had taken to waving flags of his native Dominican Republic and taping placards bearing the letter "K" (the letter used in a scorebook to designate a strikeout) onto the wall every time Pedro struck out a batter, provided Pedro with an overwhelming rush of emotion.

And he didn't disappoint his cheering fans. Pedro pitched the first two innings, striking out five of the six batters he faced, overpowering some of the National League's best hitters with his assortment of superstar pitches. For his efforts, Pedro was named the Most Valuable Player of the All-Star Game.

The season did not go totally smoothly, however. After the All-Star Game, Pedro felt stiffness behind his right shoulder, forcing him to miss games for two weeks. Another physical problem cropped up in the first round of the American League playoffs, when Pedro had to leave his Game One start against the Cleveland Indians after four innings because of a muscle strain in his back.

But Pedro's storybook season had a triumphant personal ending to it. Pedro, ignoring the muscle strain and the inability to throw as hard as he normally can, pitched six innings of shutout relief in the Red Sox' win in a decisive Game Five against the Indians.

In his only start of the American League Championship Series, against the Yankees, Pedro shut out New York on two hits over seven innings of Boston's 3-1 win, the only victory for the Red Sox in the series.

As outstanding start followed outstanding start, manager Jimy Williams and pitching coach Joe Kerrigan were running out of words trying to describe and compare Pedro's games to each other. "Do you people realize what you're seeing?" Williams would ask the media after yet another spectacular Pedro game. "Do you realize how special this young man is and how special it is what he's doing?"

Kerrigan realized it, but even he admitted it wasn't until after the season when he was able to sit back and try to put Pedro's magical season in perspective. "It was pretty special. It's something you're probably not going to see again, or something that happens once every 25 years in the game."

"In the winter . . . it seemed like every week or every two weeks someone would come out with some numbers as to what he did. And as the winter grew on, his season became more impressive," said Kerrigan the following spring.

Kerrigan pointed out some of those numbers. The opposition hit only .204 against Pedro. When the opposition pushed a runner as far as second base, called having a runner in scoring position, Pedro struck out 72 of the 167 batters he faced in those situations. He struck out 167 of the 366 batters he faced. And 66 percent of Pedro's pitches were strikes.

Even his teammates admired what Pedro did, especially because Pedro was, above all, a team player, and not just someone who was concerned with his own personal statistics. "I'm glad he's on our team," said All-Star shortstop Nomar Garciaparra. "He's a tremendous pitcher. He's fun to watch. It's like an honor to watch him pitch. There are times you become a fan when he's out there pitching."

Bret Saberhagen, who had two Cy Young Awards, was impressed, too. "It was awesome," said Saberhagen of Pedro's season. "It was almost as enjoyable as when I pitched. When I pitch, I feel that excitement, whether I was throwing a shutout or I'd given up four runs. That's my enjoyment. Watching him pitch was close to what I get out of it when I'm out there. He's fun to watch."

It is fun to watch unless you're on the other side, having to step into the batter's box. The Yankees, on that day in mid-September, didn't have much fun, though they were filled with admiration after Pedro's 1-hit, 17-strikeout gem.

"Awesome. That's as good as you can throw," said Yankee catcher Joe Girardi. "You have to look for one pitch in one location against him and hope you get it," said first baseman Tino Martinez. "I didn't get anything to hit. He was inside and outside with his location, one time up I got changeups, another time

No MVP Award?

Pedro was the starting pitcher for the American League in the 1999 All-Star Game. He struck out five of the six batters he faced in the two innings he played, which earned him the Most Valuable Player Award for the game.

I got all fastballs. He was all over the place with all of his pitches, for strikes. It was tough to get a good swing. He was pumped up. He never let up." Paul O'Neill sighed, "If he pitched like that every game, he'd never lose."

In 1999 it seemed as if Pedro Martinez never lost, notching a season for the ages that made him arguably the most valuable player in the league, even if he didn't win the official award.

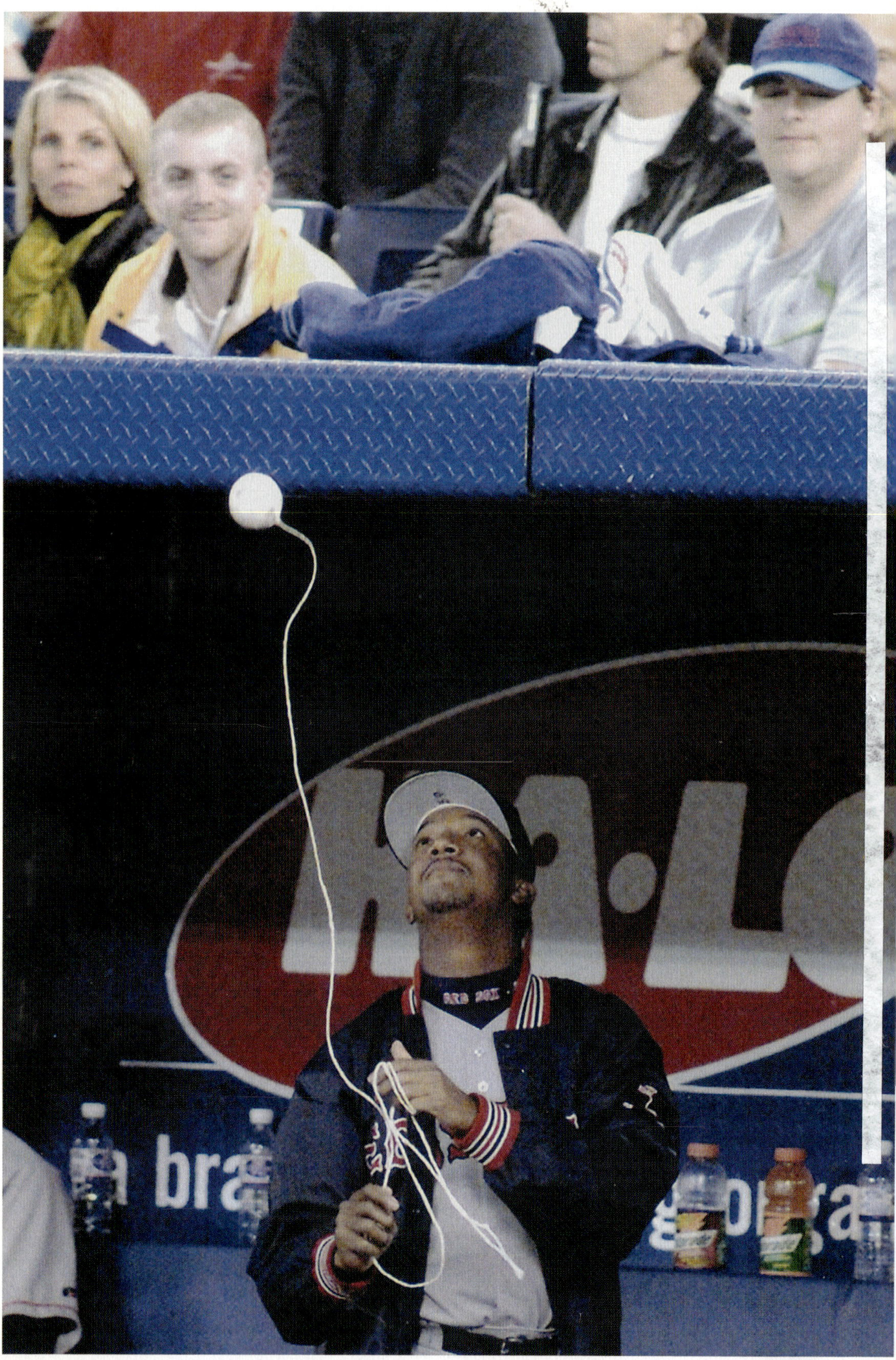

THE TWO SIDES OF PEDRO

An impish grin lit up his face as Pedro Martinez strolled into the Boston Red Sox clubhouse one day during the 1999 season. He bounded playfully over to a teammate's locker, reached in, and pulled out his teammate's uniform pants. Pedro was not a big man, especially as professional athletes go. At his heaviest, he weighed about 180 pounds that season, so his own uniform pants had a small waist. His teammate was much larger, one of the heavier players in the league. When Pedro held up the pants and spread them out, his trademark smile could be seen from every corner of the large room.

When Pedro stepped into the pants, it looked as if he had jumped into a circus tent. That's how large the pants were compared to Pedro's body. They were so large he could have placed both legs in one of the pant legs. Instead, he put on the pants one leg at a time, and then stumbled around the locker room, the pants almost falling to his knees. All the while, Pedro was laughing. His teammates were howling, too.

His teammates had become used to Pedro's behavior off the field. Pedro was a jokester, a fun-loving young man

---

Pedro teases fans with a baseball tied to a string while watching the game from the dugout. He's a fierce competitor on the mound, and a fun-loving jokester when not in the game.

who enjoyed making his teammates laugh.

One day, he put on a rubber Yoda mask, a resemblance of the old, wrinkled character in the movie, *Star Wars*, and wore it in the dugout briefly during a Red Sox game. Another time, Pedro was talking so much, telling jokes, that his teammates took athletic tape and taped first his mouth shut, and then they taped him to a post in the Boston dugout.

His teammates were laughing, but Pedro was unable to laugh because his mouth was taped shut. His expressive eyes were smiling because Pedro loved to have fun.

When it was Pedro's day to pitch, however, his personality changed drastically. Pitching was no joking matter. Pedro was serious when it came to performing on the mound. Fun on the mound came in the form of pitching well, competing at the highest level he possibly could.

His eyes would reflect his serious attitude when he was pitching. They were steely and narrowed in concentration. His brow was furrowed as this pitching master, as intelligent on the mound as he was off of it, prepared himself for the day's battle.

Pedro showed a lot of confidence on the field. His attitude sometimes bordered on cockiness, just one of the qualities that made him such a great pitcher. He was as strong mentally as he was physically. In his mind, there was no way he was going to be beaten.

He knew that he wouldn't win every game he pitched. That wasn't possible. As he would put it, "I'm only human. I'm going to give it up sometimes."

Pedro approached each game as if it were a valuable gem for him to protect. He viewed the opposition as people trying to take away the

THE TWO SIDES OF PEDRO

Pedro's teammates appreciate his sense of humor and often join in on the fun. Here, pitcher Bret Saberhagen tapes Pedro to a pole in the dugout after hearing one too many of his jokes.

gem from him, and Pedro wasn't about to let that happen without a fight. Pedro may have been small, but he wasn't about to back down from anyone or any situation on a ballfield.

It was a much different side of Pedro than the one he displayed off the field. And it was this tough, competitive side that sometimes got him into trouble on the field with the opposition.

One part of his game especially angered enemy batters. Overall, they respected Pedro's pitching talents, his consistent 95-mile-an-hour fastball, his masterful changeup, and his virtually unhittable breaking ball. But occasionally, Pedro would hit a batter.

Pedro, who had one season in which he struck out 313 batters and walked only 37, at times would exhibit a sudden loss of his customary pin-point control, resulting in inside pitches that hit batters.

Several times in his career, Pedro hit batters who became so enraged they charged the mound, trying to tackle and punch Pedro. While pitching in Montreal, he picked up the reputation as a "headhunter," as someone who would intentionally throw at batters. Whether or not it was true, it was a reputation that stuck.

In the National League, when Pedro was at bat, he would be hit by the opposing pitcher in retaliation for hitting batters on that pitcher's team. Once, Pedro charged the mound and was given an eight-game suspension.

In the American League, a designated hitter is used for the pitcher's spot in the lineup, meaning the pitcher never has to bat. That, say some hitters, gives pitchers even more courage to throw at hitters because they never have to get into the batter's box, facing retaliation from the opposing pitcher.

Pedro, though, would say he had to pitch to the inner half of the plate to make him a more effective pitcher. If he didn't, then the hitter could lean over the plate and cover more of its 17 inches, making him a more effective hitter. Twice during the 2000 season, Pedro was involved in situations where his actions triggered bench-clearing incidents. One time resulted in a five-game suspension for Pedro. In the other, he escaped injury and nearly pitched the first no-hitter of his career.

The first such incident occurred in Cleveland on April 30. The Cleveland Indians were not overly fond of Pedro as a pitcher anyway, not after his heroics in knocking them out of the playoffs the previous season. Pedro threw a pitch close to the head of young Cleveland catcher Einar Diaz, causing him to spin away and fall to the ground a split-second before a fastball would have struck his helmet. The Indians were angry. Earlier in the game, Diaz had hit two doubles off Pedro, so the Indians thought Pedro was throwing at Diaz.

In baseball, there is an unwritten code of etiquette. You throw at one of our players, we throw at one of yours. Also you don't throw at the head. That is one of the unwritten rules. So when Boston came to bat the next time, Cleveland pitcher Charles Nagy hit Jose Offerman with a pitch on the leg.

The players from each team raced onto the field, but no punches were thrown.

When the Indians came to bat next, Pedro hit Roberto Alomar on the rear end. Again the benches and bullpens emptied. Again, no punches were thrown, but Pedro was ejected from the game.

"It's all part of the game," said Pedro after the game. "These are things that happen. I have a job to do, and you have to do the job the right way. I'm not saying I wanted to hit Alomar. He's one of the best players in the game. He understands the game. If he was on my team, I'd do it for him, too. Any team that feels it will retaliate against us, we will retaliate."

A similar situation occurred at Tropicana Field on August 29. The Tampa Bay Devil Rays' first batter of the game was Gerald Williams. And with the count of one ball and two strikes on Williams, Pedro threw one of his patented 95-mile-an-hour fastballs toward the inside part of the plate. The ball zeroed in on Williams, hitting him on the hand. For Pedro, who had walked 27 batters to that point in the season, the hit batsman was his 14th, tops in the American League.

After hesitating for a few seconds, feeling the pain, Williams charged the mound, trying to get at Pedro. Williams swung his arms at Pedro, trying to land a punch as Pedro backpedaled on the mound.

In seconds, there were several players scuffling on the mound. Pedro emerged unhurt. Williams was ejected from the game. Pedro said he was surprised to see Williams racing angrily to the mound. "It's not like I haven't been charged before. I've been through that many times, but it was only the fourth pitch of the game, a fastball I wanted to get inside," said Pedro.

This time, unlike the game in Cleveland, Pedro maintained his cool. He was well aware that, with the Red Sox still trying to earn a playoff spot, he couldn't afford to do anything after the first incident to get tossed out of the game and face a possible suspension. His team needed him too much.

Pedro not only regained his composure, he used whatever emotions he may have been feeling from the brawl to make him an even better pitcher. After hitting Williams, Pedro retired the next 24 batters he faced — no walks, no hits, no more hit batsmen.

Entering the ninth inning, Pedro had a chance to pitch a no-hitter. The Devil Rays' John Flaherty spoiled that dream by lining a single, leading off the ninth, but Pedro won the game, 8-0, on a one-hitter, and earned even more admiration from his teammates and manager.

"I normally stay focused, but after that incident, I wanted to remain calm," Pedro said after the game. "The thing I wanted to do was win the game rather than try to plunk anybody or hit anybody. It was more important for me to win the game. I can not afford to retaliate, get thrown out and get suspended. I can't be stupid."

Manager Jimy Williams appreciated Pedro's control on this night. "Teams can try to rattle him, but things don't bother him," said manager Jimy Williams. "He keeps them in perspective. Someone has to be in control of his mental faculties out there, and he is. You factor in his (pitching) stuff and that's what puts him in that upper echelon of pitchers. That's how great this kid is."

Pedro always had a grasp of the right way to do things on the diamond. "Baseball is so old. Things have been going on in the game. We play as a team. We fight as a team. We go down as a team. We win as a team. It's part of the game. There's no crying in baseball," said Pedro.

Pedro has been called a "headhunter" by opposing teams because he has a tendency to hit batters with his pitches. Pedro says his hits are accidental, and a result of his style of pitching to the inside of the plate. There have been many times when batters have charged at Pedro on the mound after being hit with a pitch to retaliate with a punch.

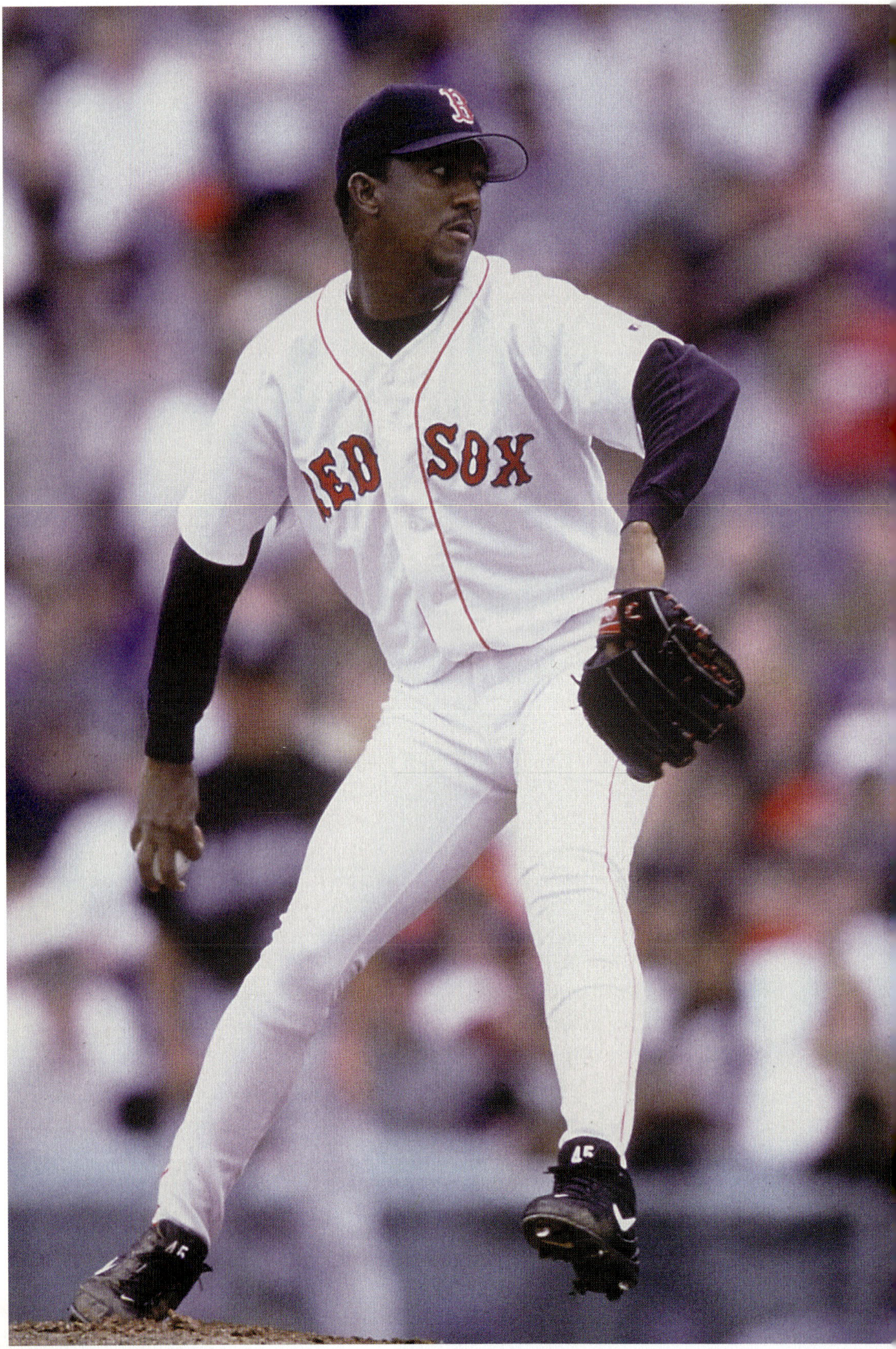
SOX

6

CAN YOU TOP THIS?

Pedro Martinez had a spectacular season in 1999. When he arrived at spring training camp in Fort Myers, Florida, in February 2000, the questions were predictable.

He was asked, "Can you have just as good a season as you had in 1999? Can you do even better?" Pedro considered the questions and smiled. "Only God knows that," said Pedro. "I'm not saying I can do it, and I'm not saying I can't. I don't have anything to prove. I'll just have to go do my job and see what happens."

Pedro went out and did his job for the Boston Red Sox in the 2000 season. And while his final numbers for the year weren't quite up to his American League-leading 23-4 record, 2.07 earned-run average, and 313 strikeouts in 1999—and his All-Star Game performance that won him the Most Valuable Player Award—arguments could be made that Pedro had an even better year in 2000.

Pedro went 18-6, leading the league in earned-run average (1.74) and strikeouts (284) in 2000.

Pedro was the unanimous winner of the Cy Young Award for the second year in a row. He was voted as the best pitcher in the American League by the Baseball Writers' Association

---

Pedro's spectacular season in 1999 put the pressure on him to repeat his performance in 2000. In the face of this kind of challenge, Pedro's competitive nature kicked in and lead him to his second straight season as the unanimous Cy Young Award winner.

of America, named number one on each of the 28 ballots. Pedro thus became the league's first back-to-back winner to be voted the award unanimously each time.

"I think this year was equally good," said Pedro upon learning he had received his second straight Cy Young, about a month after his 29th birthday. "I wouldn't choose one above the other. Each one is special and equally as important. This is just as special as last year," said Pedro, who also won a Cy Young Award when he was with Montreal, in 1997.

"It's always special to win a Cy Young. You just don't get as impressed as much as the first time, but it is equally as special," he said. While the always down-to-earth Pedro may not have been overly impressed with the award, his pitching performances certainly were impressive again in 2000.

In an era in which home runs were flying out of the ballparks with regularity and runs were being scored in high numbers, Pedro's earned-run average of 1.74 was almost two runs less than the second-place finisher in the statistic, the New York Yankees' Roger Clemens, who was at 3.70. The league average was 4.90 earned runs for every nine innings.

Pedro also led the league in shutouts (4), batting average against (.167), strikeouts per nine innings (11.8), and home runs allowed per nine innings (.71).

It was just another dominant season as Pedro cemented his reputation as one of the game's best pitchers of the era, if not the very best. "He's really put together a remarkable run, as good a run in history as any pitcher," said Boston Red Sox general manager, Dan Duquette, who acquired Martinez from Montreal in a trade after the 1997 season and then signed him to a six-year, $75-million contract. "[H]e's been a great gift to the Red Sox franchise," said Duquette. "We're very proud of Pedro's accomplishment. . . . He's reached an extraordinary level at a young age."

Pedro said he appreciated being a member of the Red Sox. "It really is a great honor to be part of this great franchise and it's always a pleasure to be able to get something to bring back to Boston, to my country and to the fans," said Pedro.

He gave Red Sox fans many memorable moments during the 2000 season.

In May, Pedro allowed only two hits in Baltimore, shutting out the Orioles, 9-0, at Camden Yards. He struck out 15 that day. Later in the month, Pedro hooked up with Clemens, a four-time Cy Young winner, in one of the best pitching duels in a long time, electricity filling the air at Yankee Stadium. Pedro limited the defending World Champion New York Yankees to four hits in Boston's 2-0 victory. He struck out 9 that night.

In his next start, Pedro was nicked for only one hit in eight innings in a 3-0 win over the Cleveland Indians. Then there was the game on July 23 when Pedro shut out the Chicago White Sox, 1-0, again striking out 15 batters.

And on August 29 at Tropicana Field, Pedro came within three outs of pitching his first no-hitter. But the Tampa Bay Devil Rays' John Flaherty ruined Pedro's chance by hitting a single to right-center, leading off the ninth inning. Still, Pedro and the Sox won, 8-0, with Pedro striking out 13 batters.

Even on those rare occasions when Pedro didn't win, he was able to thrill the fans. On May 6 Pedro lost a 1-0 duel to Tampa Bay's pitcher Steve Trachsel, but Pedro struck out 17, tying his career high.

Overall, of his 29 starts, Pedro gave up more than three earned runs in a game only twice, which is a tribute to his incredible consistency.

Along the way Pedro was selected for the All-Star team for the fifth year in a row. Pedro's own selection for his best performance, however, was his worst game of the year, at least statistically. In Kansas City on August 24, Pedro had a tough time against the Royals. Of the first six batters he faced, five got hits. And there was another hit later in the inning. By the time the inning was over, Kansas City had pushed five runs across home plate against the normally invincible Pedro Martinez.

Pedro, an intense competitor, stalked to the dugout when the inning was over. He sat on the bench, his pride ruffled a bit, but his competitiveness still burning fiercely.

In the next inning, Pedro surrendered a home run to Mike Sweeney, a blast that gave the Royals a 6-1 lead. Still, Pedro was not willing to just pack it in, shrug it off as just one of those nights, and come out of the game. He knew the team needed him to pitch deep into the game on this night because the relief pitchers had been used a lot in recent times, and they were tired. So Pedro kept pitching, his typically dogged determination and confidence fueling his effort, not to mention his sizzling fastball, devastating changeup and baffling curveball.

Pedro pitched six more innings after having been battered over the first two. In those final six innings he pitched, Pedro did not allow any runs. Indeed, he gave up only one more hit, holding the Royals at bay while the Red Sox' offense finally came alive, ultimately winning the game, 9-7, in 10 innings.

"Those last six innings were tremendous," marveled manager Jimy Williams. "He could have bagged it, but he didn't. To me, that was impressive. He figured it out. That's Pedro."

It is said that in adversity you find out the true measure of a person. In this case, Pedro suffered through uncharacteristic adversity on the diamond, and he rose above it, which is why he chose this as his best start of the year. "I'm more proud of this game than most of the games I've started," said Pedro after the game. "I'm really proud of this game because I had to use my mind and use everything I have within me to stay in that long and battle that team."

"It was a day I didn't feel too good early in the game. I didn't have anything going early in the game and they were at their best. But I was able to survive. I gave the team what it needed, some help for the bullpen," he said.

Throughout almost all of the 2000 season, Pedro gave the Sox what they needed. But there were a few problems with his health that limited him. He missed one start in early June because of a strained oblique muscle, and from late June to the middle of July that strained muscle kept him on the sidelines. In mid-August, a little stiffness in his valuable right shoulder forced him to come out of a game early. On the whole, though, it was another great season for Pedro Martinez.

Unfortunately, it was not a perfect season. The Red Sox did not make it into the playoffs, a fact that made winning the Cy Young a little less fulfilling for the team-oriented pitcher. "I'd probably trade this award for the World Series or the chance to play in it," said Pedro, whose Red Sox finished

Even when facing adversity, such as when he gave up five hits against the first six batters in a a game against the Royals, Pedro always comes through. When other pitchers would have given up, Pedro persevered and lead the Red Sox to the win.

Pedro signs autographs for his young fans. When asked if he could repeat his outstanding performances in 1999 and 2000 yet again, Pedro replied, "with a big try, it's possible." It's this attitude, along with his amazing pitching abilities, that has made Pedro such a success in major league baseball.

second to the Yankees in their division. "We played pretty good this season. . . . We shouldn't be disappointed. . . . We did the best we could."

No one did it any better than Pedro Martinez. Again. Even as he was accepting his 2000 Cy Young Award, Pedro was just waiting for the questions featuring a familiar theme.

The media asked, "Can you top what you did in 1999 and 2000? Is a third straight Cy Young Award possible?"

"If I can stay healthy, I think it's possible," said Pedro. "If you guarantee [my] health, I'll guarantee you a big try. And with a big try, it's possible."

That's what Pedro Martinez had been proving since those early days as a youngster in Manoguayabo of the Dominican Republic, playing baseball whenever he could with his brothers Nelson, Ramon and Jesus.

With a big try, anything is possible.

CHRONOLOGY

1971   Born on October 25 in Manoguayabo, Dominican Republic.

1988   Signed to free-agent baseball contract by the Los Angeles Dodgers.

1990   Begins professional career in Great Falls, Montana; named to Pioneer League All-Star team.

1991   Pitches in the Dodgers' minor-league system for Bakersfield, San Antonio, and Albuquerque. Named the *Sporting News* Minor League Player of the Year. Named top right-handed pitcher by *Baseball America.*

1992   Selected for Triple A All-Star Game while pitching for Albuquerque, the Dodgers' top minor league team. Makes major league debut for the Dodgers on September 24, pitching two scoreless innings against the Cincinnati Reds.

1993   Begins the season in Albuquerque, but is promoted to Los Angeles on April 11. Earns first major league win on May 5, against the Mets. On November 19, traded from the Los Angeles Dodgers to the Montreal Expos.

1994   On June 9, has first major league complete game and shutout against New York Mets.

1995   On June 3 in San Diego, pitches 9 perfect innings, retiring all 27 batters.

1996   Selected to National League All-Star team. On August 29, pitches against his brother, Ramon, marking only the sixth time in major league history that brothers have started against each other.

1997   Selected to National League All-Star team. Wins Cy Young Award. First Latin pitcher to strike out 300. Named Sporting News National League pitcher of the year. On November 18, traded from Montreal to the Boston Red Sox.

1998   Selected to the American League All-Star team. On April 11 records his 1,000th major league strikeout.

1999   Selected to American League All-Star team. Starts All-Star Game and wins the game's Most Valuable Player Award; wins American League Cy Young Award. Finishes second in American League Most Valuable Player Award voting. Named Associated Press Major League Player of the Year. Wins American League Pitcher of the Month honor four times, the first person ever to do so.

2000   Selected to American League All-Star team. Wins American League Cy Young Award, only the seventh pitcher in the major leagues to win as many as three Cy Young Awards.

ACCOMPLISHMENTS

1991	*Sporting News* Minor League Player of the Year.
	Baseball America Top Minor League Right-handed Pitcher
1997	National League Cy Young Award
	Sporting News National League Pitcher of the Year
1998	1,000th Major League Strikeout
1999	American League Cy Young Award
	American League All-Star Game Most Valuable Player
	American League Pitcher of the Month (four times)
	Associated Press Major League Player of the Year
2000	American League Cy Young Award

FURTHER READING

Gallagher, Mike. *Pedro Martinez*. Maryland: Mitchell Lane Publishers, 1999.

Shalin, Mike. *Pedro Martinez: Throwing Strikes*. Illinois: Sports Publishing, Inc., 1999

Stewart, Mark. *Pedro Martinez: Pitcher Perfect*. New York: Children's Press, 2000.

INDEX

Abreu, Paulino Jaime (father), 29
Albuquerque, New Mexico, 19, 21
Alomar, Roberto, 49
Alou, Felipe, 30
Alou brothers, 30
American League All-Star Game, 39-40, 53, 56
American League Championship Series, 41, 42-43
American League Division Championships, 7-15, 40-41
American League Pitcher of the Month, 39
Bakersfield, California, 19
Baltimore Orioles, 55
Boston Red Sox, 25, 27, 32-35, 54-55
Chicago White Sox, 55
Clemens, Roger, 54, 55
Cleveland Indians, 7-15, 40-41, 48-49, 55
Cy Young Award
 American League, 25, 39, 53-54, 57, 58
 National League, 23, 32, 54
Davis, Chil, 37
DeShields, Delino, 22
Diaz, Einar, 49
Dominican Republic, 17-18, 27-35, 40
Duquette, Dan, 54-55
Flaherty, John, 50, 55

Garciaparra, Nomar, 42
Girardi, Joe, 42
Great Falls, Montana, 19
Houston Astros, 32
Kansas City Royals, 56-57
Kerrigan, Joe, 11, 14, 15, 41-42
Knoblauch, Chuck, 37
Little League All-Star team, 29
Los Angeles Dodgers, 18, 19, 21-22, 25, 32
Marichal, Juan, 30, 32
Martinez, Jesus (brother), 17-18, 58
Martinez, Nelson (brother), 17-18, 58
Martinez, Pedro
 appearance of, 9, 18, 20, 45
 and attitude towards pitching, 46-47
 with Boston Red Sox, 25, 27, 54-55
 childhood of, 17-18, 29, 31, 58
 and church in Dominican Republic, 27-28
 education of, 19, 32
 family of, 17-20, 22, 24-25, 28-29
 and first major league win, 21
 as highest-paid pitcher, 27, 54-55

and hitting batters, 11, 47-51
 as jokester, 45-46
 with Los Angeles Dodgers, 19, 21-22, 32
 and major league debut, 19, 21
 with minor league, 19-21
 with Montreal Expos, 22-25, 27, 30, 48, 54-55
 and 1999 season, 7-15, 25, 37-43, 53
 and striking out 305 hitters, 22
 and 2000 season, 25, 47-51, 53-58
Martinez, Ramon (brother), 11, 12, 17-21, 22, 24-25, 28, 58
Martinez, Tino, 42-43
Montreal Expos, 22-25, 27, 30, 48, 54-55
Morgan, Dr. William, 11
Most Valuable Player of the All-Star Game, 40, 53
Nagy, Charles, 49
New York Yankees, 37-39, 41, 42-43, 55, 58
Offerman, Jose, 49
Ohio Dominican College, 32

O'Leary, Troy, 14
O'Neill, Paul, 38, 43
Rodriquez, Ivan "Pudge," 38
Saberhagen, Bret, 42
San Antonio, Texas, 19
Sosa, Sammy, 28
Sporting News Minor League Player of the Year, 19
Tampa Bay Devil Rays, 49-51, 55
Thome, Jim, 11
Torre, Joe, 38, 39
Trachsel, Steve, 55
Triple A All-Star Game, 19
Valentin, John, 11
Varitek, Jason, 11
Vizquel, Omar, 8-9, 14
Williams, Gerald, 49-50
Williams, Jimy, 10, 14, 41, 51, 56

Photo Credits:

2: Duane Burleson/AP/Wide World Photos
6: Phil Long/AP/Wide World Photos
9: Jim Mone/AP/Wide World Photos
13: Reuters NewMedia Inc./Corbis
15: AFP/Corbis
16: Otto Greule/AllSport USA
20: Reuters/Brian Snyder/Archive Photos
23: Elca Hacch/AllSport USA
24: Stephen Dunn/AllSport USA
26: Lynne Sladky/AP/Wide World Photos
30: Paul Chiasson/AP/Wide World Photos
33: Julia Malakie/AP/Wide World Photos
34: AP/Wide World Photos
36: Otto Greule/AllSport USA
40: Reuters NewMedia Inc./Corbis
43: Reuters NewMedia Inc./Corbis
44: Kevin Frayer/AP/Wide World Photos
47: Winslow Townson/AP/Wide World Photos
51: AFP/Corbis
52: Ezra Shaw/AllSport USA
57: Steven Senne/AP/Wide World Photos
58: Reuters/Jim Bourg/Archive Photos

Cover photo: Reuters/Brian Snyder/Archive Photos

ABOUT THE AUTHOR

STEVEN KRASNER has been a sports writer for the Providence Journal since 1975. He has been a beat reporter for the Boston Red Sox since 1986. Steven is the author of children's books and has been performing an interactive writing program called "Nudging the Imagination" in classrooms and at conferences since 1985. Steven and his wife, Susan Oclassen, live in East Greenwich, Rhode Island, with their three children, Amy, Jeffery, and Emily.